CW00540793

CHOICE SELECTORS RECOMMENDATION SPECIAL COMMENDATION	JO CLEMENT & ROY McFARLANE
TRANSLATION SELECTOR	SHIVANEE RAMLOCHAN
PAMPHLET SELECTORS	YOUSIF M. QASMIYEH & ALYCIA PIRMOHAMED
CONTRIBUTORS	SOPHIE O'NEILL MEGAN ROBSON LEDBURY CRITICS
EDITORIAL & DESIGN	ALICE KATE MULLEN

Poetry Book Society Memberships

Choice

4 Books a Year: 4 Choice books & 4 *Bulletins* (UK £65, Europe £85, ROW £120)

World

8 Books: 4 Choices, 4 Translation books & 4 *Bulletins* (£98, £160, £190)

Complete

24 Books: 4 Choices, 16 Recommendations, 4 Translations & 4 *Bulletins* (£230, £290, £360)

Single copies of the *Bulletin* £12.99

Cover Artwork: 'The Side Newcastle' by Anthony Marshall
www.thebiscuitfactory.com

Copyright Poetry Book Society and contributors. All rights reserved.
ISBN 9781913129729   ISSN 0551-1690

Supported using public funding by
ARTS COUNCIL ENGLAND

MIX
Paper | Supporting responsible forestry
FSC® C014866

Poetry Book Society | Milburn House | Dean Street | Newcastle upon Tyne | NE1 1LF
0191 230 8100 | enquiries@poetrybooksociety.co.uk

WWW.POETRYBOOKS.CO.UK

CONTENTS

CHOICE

Ian Duhig • *An Arbitrary Light Bulb* • Picador

RECOMMENDATIONS

Tim Tim Cheng • *The Tattoo Collector* • Nine Arches Press
Hasib Hourani • *rock flight* • Prototype
Joshua Idehen • *Songbook: Collected Works* • Bad Betty Press
Helen Ivory • *Constructing a Witch* • Bloodaxe Books

SPECIAL COMMENDATION

Ruth Padel • *Girl* • Chatto & Windus

TRANSLATION CHOICE

Kim Hyesoon • *Phantom Pain Wings* • And Other Stories
Translated by Don Mee Choi

PAMPHLET CHOICE

Morag Smith • *National Song* • Broken Sleep Books

LETTER FROM THE PBS

Welcome to the Winter *Bulletin*. You will find no schmaltzy Christmas themes here – this is a hard-hitting Choice and group of selections which take us on a historic and global journey. As ever, we hope these selections inspire, educate, and provoke thought and discussion.

We decided that we should give more background and attention to those amazing poet-selectors who read all the quarterly submissions and are brave enough to proclaim their Selections. I know having access to all that poetry in advance of publication is the stuff of dreams to most of us, however having to sift, assess, select and review is not an easy task, and not one that everyone is comfortable doing, so we are hugely grateful to the dedication and professionalism of the poets, writers and broadcasters we work with. Our selectors tend to rotate every two years and at this point we are saying thank you and farewell to Jo Clement and Roy McFarlane who are going out with a bang with a brilliant selection of poets in this Winter *Bulletin*. See more on our poet partners in the next two pages.

Those of you with eagle eyes will have spotted that in giving more space to the people who make this *Bulletin* we have dropped the full list of titles publishing in the quarter in this print edition. This is still a key part of our work, we can't review all titles, but please note all books and pamphlets are fully listed and available on our website. If you would like the listings emailed or posted to you, please just let us know. It was becoming harder and harder to squeeze all the books in and make them readable to the naked eye!

Although there is no Christmas theme in the *Bulletin*, this is the time when we like to remind members and our book-buying friends to give the gift of poetry! We have curated our usual poetic Christmas Gift Guide, featuring lots of lovely poetry book presents, and don't forget you can gift a membership to friends and family too. Please be assured that any extra books or memberships you buy helps to support contemporary poetry and poets.

SOPHIE O'NEILL
PBS & INPRESS DIRECTOR

MEET THE PBS SELECTORS

— VICTORIA KENNEFICK —
— 2025 BOOK SELECTOR —

Victoria Kennefick lives in Kerry. Her debut *Eat or We Both Starve* (Carcanet) won the Seamus Heaney First Collection Poetry Prize and a Dalkey Book Festival Award. She was Poet-in-Residence at the Yeats Society Sligo 2022-24. *Egg/Shell* won the PBS Spring 2024 Choice.

— YOMI ŞODE —
— 2025 BOOK SELECTOR —

Yomi Şode is a Nigerian British writer. His debut *Manorism* (Penguin) was shortlisted for the Rathbones Folio and the T.S. Eliot Prize. He won the Brunel International African Poetry Prize 2021 and a Jerwood Compton Fellowship. His libretto *Remnants* premiered on BBC Radio 3 and his play *And breathe…* was performed at the Almeida.

— JO CLEMENT —
— 2024 BOOK SELECTOR —

Dr Jo Clement is a working-class poet based in Newcastle. A Northern Writers' Award winner, she teaches Creative Writing at Northumbria University. She is Managing Editor of *Butcher's Dog*. Her debut *Outlandish* (Bloodaxe) confronts Romantic impressions of British Gypsy, Roma, and Traveller ethnicity.

— ROY McFARLANE —
— 2024 BOOK SELECTOR —

Roy McFarlane is the National Canal Laureate, former Birmingham Poet Laureate and Starbucks' Poet in Residence. He has published *Beginning With Your Last Breath*, *The Healing Next Time*, which was shortlisted for the Ted Hughes Award and *Living by Troubled Waters* (Nine Arches Press).

Meet the team of expert poet-selectors who curate the quarterly PBS selections for you....

— SHIVANEE RAMLOCHAN —
— TRANSLATION SELECTOR —

— ARJI MANUELPILLAI —
— PODCAST HOST —

Shivanee Ramlochan is a Trinidadian writer. Her debut *Everyone Knows I Am a Haunting* (Peepal Tree Press) was shortlisted for the Forward Prize. Her poems have been anthologised in *100 Queer Poems* (Faber); *After Sylvia* (Nine Arches Press) and *Across Borders: An Anthology of New Poetry from the Commonwealth* (Verve Poetry Press).

Arji Manuelpillai published his debut pamphlet *Mutton Rolls* with Out-Spoken Press. He is a member of Malika's Poetry Kitchen and was a Jerwood Arvon Mentee. Arji's debut *Improvised Explosive Device* was published by Penned in the Margins. He was our last Pamphlet Selector and hosts the PBS podcast every quarter.

— YOUSIF M. QASMIYEH —
— PAMPHLET SELECTOR —

— ALYCIA PIRMOHAMED —
— PAMPHLET SELECTOR —

Born and educated in Baddawi refugee camp in Lebanon, Yousif M. Qasmiyeh is a poet and translator with a doctorate in English Literature from the University of Oxford. His debut *Writing the Camp* (Broken Sleep Books) was a PBS Recommendation and shortlisted for the Ondaatje Prize, followed by *Eating the Archive* (Broken Sleep Books).

Alycia Pirmohamed is the author of *Another Way to Split Water*, a PBS Recommendation, and *Hinge,* which was a Pamphlet Choice. Her nonfiction debut *A Beautiful and Vital Place* won the 2023 Nan Shepherd Prize. She teaches at the University of Cambridge and co-founded the Scottish BPOC Writers Network.

TEAM PBS

5

Image: Bob Hamilton

IAN DUHIG

Ian Duhig FRSL became a full-time writer after working with homeless people for fifteen years. He has since published eight collections of poetry, held several fellowships including at Trinity College Dublin, won the Forward Prize for Best Single Poem, the National Poetry Competition twice and his *New and Selected Poems* was awarded the 2022 Hawthornden Prize for Literature. A Cholmondeley Award recipient, Duhig has worked on a wide range of collaborations from Pre-Baroque music with the Clerks to jazz-rock with Springtime, from visual art to social projects including with Leeds Irish Health and Homes and Refugee Action Bradford.

AN ARBITRARY LIGHT BULB

PICADOR | £12.99 | PBS PRICE £9.75

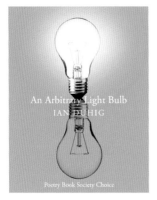

An Arbitrary Light Bulb is the ultimate 'Ars Poetica' in defence of poetry and the practice of being a poet, in essence a meditation on this beautiful art. Duhig invites us to walk with him under the Lantern of Demosthenes to find pebbles of inspiration which make us aware of the gift given to poets.

In Duhig's eyes the poem is elusive, or within a room to be found in another room ('Poem beginning with a Line from Ashbery'), always "preparing to happen or not":

'A poem is a pheasant', Wallace Stevens wrote;
it makes footprints like time's arrows pointing
backwards, from here to those I once followed
over new snow till they suddenly stopped dead.

We encounter light bulb moments as we look back at his life; as an altar boy, a student, or recalling an uncle teaching him about piseogs "old Irish country spells of vengeance". Certainly Duhig is a master craftsman leaving readers spellbound by form, rhyme and beat. He's enamoured by the white space, as though it were hallowed ground, and silence were divine.

Duhig has always shined a light, borne witness to the marginalised; navies, miners, road-makers, the homeless and social injustice. From his Dad to 'An Aroko for David Oluwale', he finds a room to explore all their memories.

draw David's Christian ghost into Oshun's arms,
water Goddess with a name of water, that he too
might step into the true meaning of his name,
borne back to Africa where the river of us all rose.

We find ourselves on solid ground with Duhig's writing, everything is dug, or mined, and if it worms itself to the surface or tunnels though his mind, he writes it. If it forms into something, so be it, and if it doesn't, it's still a gift to be sitting under an arbitrary light bulb.

SELECTOR'S COMMENT

ROY McFARLANE

IAN DUHIG

Statistically, I should be dead. This was a major inspiration (pace my COPD) for this new book. Named after the commonest design of household lamps, "an arbitrary light bulb", as electricians called them in an Ironmongers where I worked: the paradox of that name being commonly-unknown suggested it as an image of all the overlooked – if also, inevitably – inspiration, life and death.

The book is light and dark, formal and free – like my dual nationalities: close, yet poles apart. 1950s working-class Irish-immigrants' children were over-represented in physical and mental ill-health figures, including for early death. I'm one of only three still-living from my family's eleven children, and not the youngest. A poor student, I left school early to do manual and casual work.

Good grades at night-class A levels got me into Geoffrey Hill's University of Leeds, an overlooked, polarised city, as its Remain vote demonstrated: for conflicted poets, a good fit. I studied English Literature, recalling Irish poetry my mother shared while cooking which flowed between speech and song. I cherish memories of home but, perhaps insecure, eviction stories and homelessness resonated with me (I worked in the sector for fifteen years immediately after university). My book reflects this but more: humour, mundane wonders, fantasy – dog-shit bags ripening on branches, forgotten birdsong electrifying from new hearing aids, a heavily-intoxicated worm's adventure. For Kafka, death is the point of life, a point *An Arbitrary Light Bulb* plugs into: if my current was variable, even blackouts proved illuminating in paradoxical ways.

Celan's book *Microliths* analyses poems as paradoxes, how rhyme gathers "sense and countersense": a paradoxical craft for light and sound waves. If mine sails you under bare poles sometimes, better weather follows. Huge thanks to the PBS, its judges and readers for this book's dream launch.

IAN RECOMMENDS

Jackie Kay, *May Day* (Picador); Denise Riley, *Lurex* (Picador); Anthony Vahni Capildeo, *Polkadot Wounds* (Carcanet); Zaffar Kunial, *England's Green* (Faber); Niall Campbell, *The Island in the Sound* (Bloodaxe); Maura Dooley, *Five Fifty-Five* (Bloodaxe Books); Kayo Chingonyi, *A Blood Condition* (Chatto); Raymond Antrobus, *Signs,* Music (Picador); Paul Muldoon, *Joy in Service on Rue Tagore* (Faber); A.E. Stallings, *This Afterlife* (Carcanet); Hannah Lowe, *The Kids* (Bloodaxe); Camille Ralphs, *After You Were, I Am* (Faber); Michael Longley, *Ash Keys* (Cape); Declan Ryan, *Crisis Actor* (Faber).

PBS CHOICE

PHEASANT'S EYE

'A poem is a pheasant', Wallace Stevens wrote:
it makes footprints like time's arrows pointing
backwards, from here to those I once followed
over new snow till they suddenly stopped dead.

Fox? No foxprints. Thought fox then? I stared
at the blank page of this field so long, it grew
as foxed as I with patches where bulbs stirred,
preparing to happen or not, unmade by poetry.

What I don't know about pheasants would fill
a Borgesian library. Take down any book: open
it randomly; see the ghost of the nothing not
there and the nothing that is, the white sheet

a picnic cloth over bulbs of Narcissus poeticus,
the poet's Narcissus, known as pheasant's eye.

MY FRIENDS

a departure from Lorca's 'Desde Aqui'

this is just to say,
among other things,

I'm dead. Water sings
where willows sway –

still, I have died.
But my eyes

will remain wide
under the sky's

paper tissue,
and, if a ghost,

what star I go to,
I go to with no host.

Image: Alan Leung

TIM TIM CHENG

Tim Tim Cheng is a poet from Hong Kong, currently based between Edinburgh and London. Her pamphlet *Tapping At Glass* (Verve, 2023) explores womanhood, multilingualism, and psychogeography. Her poems have been published and anthologised in *POETRY*, *The Rialto*, *Poetry London, Our Time Is A Garden*, and elsewhere. Her latest appearances include the StAnza Poetry Festival, Hidden Door festival, Singapore Writers' Festival, and BBC Scotland. She is a WrICE fellow (awarded by RMIT University), an Ignite fellow (Scottish Book Trust), a member of the Southbank Centre's New Poets Collective 2022/23, and a mentee under the Roddy Lumsden Memorial Mentorship scheme.

THE TATTOO COLLECTOR

NINE ARCHES PRESS | £11.99 | PBS PRICE £9.00

Simmering beneath *The Tattoo Collector's* skin are the tumultuous events that have unfolded in Hong Kong in recent years. Haunted by the former Crown Colony's ghosts, the opening poem's speaker cross-examines herself and the police presence established by the British government. Here, the violent response to the Water Revolution's peaceful protestors replays through images of handcuffs, bruised faces, and bloodshot eyes ('Questions for the Police at Royal Infirmary'). The ten-part poem 'How Memory Works' confronts the free press shutdown of 2020, as a mother and daughter try to buy a pro-democracy newspaper:

> Sure they won't catch us for buying the paper?
> Mother went with me, still. Ghosts police too.
> She prayed only for me to hear.

Cheng's rebellious poems are devoted to counterculture and transport readers into transcendent experiences, such as a Mogwai performance ('Silence'). The Glaswegian band's name is a transliteration of the Cantonese 魔鬼 meaning demon. At the gig, malevolent spirits take unexpected forms as the speaker chips a tooth on a beer bottle and hears "a ringing / through my skull". '意色樓 An Id Signal' immerses the reader in a metal club's "sweat, booze, and smoke", capturing the pulse of underground movements. Increasingly, women get tattoos to prevent people trafficking because "the more / marked you are, the easier it is / to identify / you" ('Skin.Me'). In 'The Tattooist', a grandmother's "dotted" hands acknowledge how customs like tattooing once saved women from sexual slavery, whilst others, like foot binding, left immeasurable damage:

> Mallets broke bits of our bodies
> to prepare us for a husband, prevent us
> from being abducted
> as comfort women.

Tim Tim Cheng's dazzling debut counters the words and beliefs of those intergenerationally "shamed into shaming" ('Girl Ghosts'), as she finds solace from historic and contemporary injustices in the intimate space of the tattoo parlour and looks through the glass of museum collections, where:

> Blessed are the pains
> that numb other pains: I kneel on a butterfly

JO CLEMENT

SELECTOR'S COMMENT

TIM TIM CHENG

My publisher came up with my collection's title, *The Tattoo Collector*. It was then I started to see what I was doing: Tattoos, as in designs inked on our skins, as in military performances, as in drumming. Not only does the title share my name's acronym, it also etymologically splinters from my pamphlet, *Tapping At Glass* (Verve, 2023). According to the Online Etymology Dictionary, the word tattoo could be traced back to the Dutch word *taptoe* (tap "faucet of a cask" + toe "shut, to"). It means a "signal calling soldiers or sailors to quarters at night". I was also delighted to discover that my books shared names with psychological thriller and horror fictions.

When I started writing poems on tattoos, it was a small attempt to move from my usual subject matter: Hong Kong. I wanted to set a deadline for my post-2019 grief and prove that I could write something else. I did not know those poems would evolve into a body of work. While my pamphlet focused on sitting with loss, *The Tattoo Collector* took me to what that loss revealed. I also wanted to be able to recite this book by heart. I wanted some lines to live by, in case I was locked up. (Am I sounding self-important? After all, who reads English poetry in Hong Kong?) Hold that thought and laugh at me in my future retirement home.

All this led *The Tattoo Collector* to meet eros in the dark. It shapeshifted into poems on being (un)comfortable in our own skins; colonial violence; cold war rhetorics; global struggles; the meditative and collective power of the arts; land and water disputes; living between languages; travelling across Hong Kong, Scotland, London and beyond; alternative healing; family history; one-night stands; Jollibee; monkeys; too many drinks and bad tattoos...

TIM TIM RECOMMENDS

Henry Wei Leung, *Goddess of Democracy: An Occupy Lyric* (Omnidawn); Yam Gong, *Moving a Stone: Selected Poems*, co-translated by James Shea and Dorothy Tse (Zephyr Press); Derek Chung, *A Cha Chaan Teng That Does Not Exist*, translated by May Huang (Zephyr Press); Au Wah Yan, *Dreams of A Toad* (ACO Books); Edited by Eddie Tay and Jennifer Wong, *State of Play: Poets of East & Southeast Asian Heritage in Conversation* (Out-Spoken Press).

RECOMMENDATION

this skin hears one at a time

Image: Au Wah Yan

THE TATTOO COLLECTOR

Incisions, incisions, incisions –
Gloved fingers stretch my skin for the ink to set.
I'm convinced if I turn my blank slate
into a puzzle, an exhibit, you'll be looking
and not looking into me, a site for stencilling
future's blueprints. I've practised letting strangers
apply pressure on me. Elbow my shoulders
as they resist the coming of black outlines,
which safeguard every lost charm –
a swallow faces a mountain it can never reach.
Needs to needles. Blessed are the pains
that numb other pains: I kneel on a butterfly
with time's spiral as wings. Close by, a naked night-
rider gallops the pitch dark. Her eyes glow, hair flies.

HASIB HOURANI

Hasib Hourani, born in Bahrain in 1996, is a Lebanese-Palestinian writer, editor, arts worker and educator who lives in "so-called Australia". His 2021 essay *When we blink* was shortlisted in the LIMINAL and Pantera Press Nonfiction Prize and appears in the anthology, *Against Disappearance. rock flight* is his first book.

ROCK FLIGHT

PROTOTYPE | £12.99 | PBS PRICE £9.75

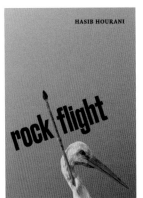

In *rock flight's* afterword Hourani says "this book uses a single narrative thread to address the systematic atrocities that Israel inflicts on Palestinians both within Palestine and across the diaspora". The collection is divided into seven parts beginning with a mantra-like manifesto of the displaced and the dispossessed.

> "it" means the reason I am elsewhere
> "thing" means the reason I am elsewhere
> "israel" means the reason I am elsewhere
> "something" means the reason I am elsewhere

Hourani's story is the story of his grandparents fleeing in 1948, children being born stateless to refugees, holding five different passports, forever being elsewhere and never attaining Palestinian citizenship. Hourani is imaginative, passionate and witty as he exposes the fault line of occupation that reverberates over generations, over lands and across a diaspora. Raw and unflinching, we find ourselves "at Karameh bridge... held till nearly sunset" or writing at a residency where a ghost sleeps on his chest, "there are settler ghosts here where I am writing and they are angry as hell."

Hourani makes reference to birds, flight and migration. There are times when he spreads his words across the page, a lyrical flight of phrases and thoughts, then suddenly the writing becomes boxed, caged, or, at other times, singular statements stand alone in a sea of white space. A poet's job is to leave you shaken, to leave a resounding mark on you and Hourani has left an indelible mark:

> before the first pfeilstorch people thought birds in the winter
> were gone because they were hibernating
>
> before the first pfeilstorch people thought birds in the winter were
> gone because they were under the water and sealed with a slip of ice
>
> before the first pfeilstorch people thought birds in the winter were
> gone because they became a different kind of bird
>
> in 1822 the first pfeilstorch landed near klütz, germany with a 30-inch spear
> made of african wood pierced through its throat.

Rock flight is the poetics of the Palestinian, still elsewhere, with a spear in their throat.

ROY McFARLANE

HASIB HOURANI

rock flight is about many things: settler violence, hyper-surveillance, birds, boycotts and my family. Parts of it are quite literally haunted. Entire sections couldn't have been written if I hadn't gone somewhere else to write them down. I took my computer interstate to start and finish a chapter that remained unread and untouched for a year afterwards. The final edits were done from a high stool at the laundromat. There are words we can't bring home with us. It's perhaps for this reason that the book often uses inference to get the words across. Fixating on a recurring set of images – rocks, birds, water, flight – explicit language is hinted at, omitted or redacted. A gesture towards censorship and a consideration for my own safety, of course, but also a reclamation of language. The book is cheeky and combative. I want the reader to smirk. I want them to scrunch up a piece of paper and throw it across the room.

I made a lot of *rock flight's* final changes in September and October 2023. We couldn't have known then that the zionist entity would double down and massacre over 50,000 Palestinians in Gaza between the book's completion and its Australian release. It took four years to write this book. But the words themselves didn't change much from one draft to the next, they simply moved around: from one line to the next, from the afterword to the body. Mimicking the relentless motion of contemporary Palestinian experience.

All of this is to say, the words and stories in *rock flight* aren't new. References and accounts date as far back as 1799. I wrote a contemporary poem that contains centuries of history, and fossilised within that graft, is something eternal.

HASIB RECOMMENDS

Don Mee Choi, *DMZ Colony* (Wave Books); Cathy Linh Che, *Split* (Alice James Books); Bhanu Kapil, *Incubation: a space for monsters* (Leon Works); Nam Le, *36 Ways of Writing a Vietnamese Poem* (Simon & Schuster); Colin Herd, *Glovebox and Other Poems* (Knives Forks and Spoons Press); T.O. Bobe, *Curl* (Wakefield Press); Joanna Cho, *People Person* (Ta Herenga Waka University Press); Etel Adnan, *Shifting the Silence* (Nightboat Books); Richard Siken, *War of the Foxes* (Copper Canyon Press); Evelyn Araluen, *Dropbear* (University of Queensland Press).

every autumn and every spring half a billion birds pass over palestinian air. the air is contested, they can't get home.

EXTRACT

17. what is dawn good for?
    a. a beautiful cusp:
        i. a veil for construction
        ii. a lift for surprise
gather at dawn
five hundred gather at dawn
picket the port of oakland
block a ship and its boxes
it's morning then it's afternoon
then it's six pm and still
the ship floats bloated
in the belly of the bay

keep it heavy
        massive
leave it no choice but to spit up
                and spit out
in glorious explosion
in plains of nonexistence

Image: Agatha Powa

JOSHUA IDEHEN

Joshua Idehen is a British-born Nigerian based in Sweden. A spoken word artist, musician and facilitator, he has contributed poems to the Mercury-nominated albums *Channel The Spirits* by The Comet Is Coming, *Your Queen Is A Reptile* and the Mobo-winning *Black To The Future*, both by Sons of Kemet. More recently, he worked with LA electronic maestro Daedelus on the critically acclaimed mini LP *Holy Water Over Sons*. In 2023, he continued his journey as a solo musical artist, collaborating with producer Ludvig Parment (Saturday, Monday) on his mixtape *Learn To Swim*, released to critical acclaim and support, leading to a performance in front of the King of Sweden at the 2023 Polar Prize Award show (TV4).

RECOMMENDATION

SONGBOOK

BAD BETTY PRESS　　　|　　　£10.99　　　|　　　PBS PRICE £8.25

The role of the griot (West African storyteller) is to tell our stories, your stories, stories of truth and love. Many griots in the past travelled the land with a band, our modern-day griots are no different; Simon Armitage, Linton Kwesi Johnson and Kae Tempest, to name a few. Joshua Idehen's debut occupies that space, and with the help of QR codes we have access to his recordings and performances with the likes of Sons of Kemet. The griot and his band have entered into the white space and into the cornea of your eye. Buckle up because Joshua Idehen is no "turn-the-other-cheek house negro", as he claims in 'We're All Field Negroes Now':

> I am a field negro now, exodusing
> from wretched plains. Pour holy palm
> wine, wash away the shame

Idehen's cup runneth over with subjects like Tamir Rice, bleaching and monarchy, "your queen is not our queen. She does not see us as human." Idehen speaks his truth from a perspective many have not experienced and, in a world turned upside down, there's a necessity to hear this truth. In 'A Want (Riots 2011)' the speaker wants "to hurt your home so badly the world knows you're alive. To set something alight. To face down the law for a night."

I'm reminded of Tony Harrison's early work, as he walked through the streets and graveyards of Leeds, as Idehen walks through Hackney, Curtain Road and Grenfell in London, chasing stories that need to be told. And there's still love, a revolutionary love, in these times:

> On the ceiling, circles dance
> Above drunken circumstance
>
> She said she almost fell in love
> I swear I almost caught her

This is a debut with a raw beauty and anger, cutting deep into our ideas of being citizens of the world. No matter what your father says...

> YOU WANT TO BE A WRITER, EH?
> YOU ARE GOING TO WASTE YOUR LIFE

Keep chasing those sonnets for a living.

ROY McFARLANE

JOSHUA IDEHEN

I wrote a lot of the first third of *Songbook* ('Black Politic') in direct response to several Black Lives Matter flashpoints of 2016 to date: Philando Castile's murder brought about 'Black Says', 'Epitaph For Tamir Rice' is about the titular victim and 'We're All Field Negroes' was written after George Floyd. At the same time, I drew a lot of artistic inspiration from political songs that shaped my understanding and ambition, such as Nina Simone's 'Mississippi Goddamn'. I really loved how she bounced between deadpan humour and righteous anger; it's something I try to emulate in my own work, in particular 'Black Says'. Also DJ Jazzy Jeff and Raheem DeVaughn's 'My Peoples', The Roots' 'Something In The Way Of Things' and Childish Gambino's 'This Is America' (just because I found it so surreal. I sought to recreate that energy when I wrote 'Mum Does The Washing'). I have been privileged to work with several great musicians across jazz, electronica and left-field – Shabaka Hutchins, LOOR and Daedelus – whose works I admire and, through our collaborations, I found fertile ground for my voice and meaning.

The second section ('London') drew inspiration from my favourite spoken word and dance tracks to catalogue the last days of the night scenes I grew up in. So we're talking Maxi Jazz from his work with Faithless, The Streets, The Mitchell Brothers, Ursula Rucker, Soul II Soul, Baxter Dury and the Bootleg House tracks I never knew the names of.

The final third section ('The Personal'), contains my oldest and youngest poems, all of them responses to single lines of songs I loved. 'On Diaspora' is a response to Fela Kuti's "I no be gentleman" from the song 'Gentleman', 'On Depression' responds to Luke Temple's "Did you hurt Somebody's Feelings?" from 'Weekend Warrior' and 'Brother' came about from Fleet Foxes: "I love you, I love you, oh brother of mine", from the track 'Blue Ridge Mountains'.

JOSHUA RECOMMENDS

Peter deGraft-Johnson, The Repeat Beat Poet, *A Testament To Life And Death* (Verve Press); Yrsa Daley Ward, *Bone* (Penguin); Yomi Şode, *Manorism* (Penguin); Roger Robinson, *A Portable Paradise* (Peepal Tree Press); Tolu Agbelusi, *Locating Strongwoman* (Jacaranda Books); Alex Green, *Emergency Anthems*: For Those I Love, For Those I Love (Brooklyn Arts Press) and Antony Szmierek's song 'Seasoning'.

RECOMMENDATION

Just let black be.
Black says,
just let black be.

THE WORLD ACCORDING TO YOUR MUM DOING THE WASHING (EXTRACT)

Capitalism:
Your mum does the washing. You pay her a pound. You get her to do your mate's washing. Your mate pays you £50.

Communism:
Your mum does the washing. You do the washing. Every night you salute a photo of your dad.

Socialism:
Your mum does the washing. You do the cooking. Everyone is happy in theory.

Fascism:
Your mum does the washing under the threat of violence.

Nazism:
Your mum does the washing. You gas the laundry room.

Feudalism:
Your mum does the washing and pays you tax.

Liberalism:
You watch your mum do the washing and feel really really bad. 'Something must be done,' you say.

....

Surrealism:
The washing does your mum.

JOSHUA IDEHEN

Image: Martin Figura

HELEN IVORY

Helen Ivory is a poet and visual artist. She edits the webzine *Ink Sweat & Tears*, and teaches at UEA/National Centre for Writing online. She has published six collections with Bloodaxe Books: *The Double Life of Clocks* (2002), *The Dog in the Sky* (2006), *The Breakfast Machine* (2010), *Waiting for Bluebeard* (2013), *The Anatomical Venus* (2019), and *Constructing a Witch* (2024). *Fool's World*, a collaborative Tarot with artist Tom de Freston (Gatehouse Press), won the 2016 Saboteur Best Collaborative Work award. A US edition *Wunderkammer: New and Selected Poems* was published by MadHat in 2023. In 2024 she received a Cholmondeley Award from the Society of Authors.

CONSTRUCTING A WITCH

BLOODAXE BOOKS | £12.99 | PBS PRICE £9.75

Constructing a Witch is spellbinding. Helen Ivory's sixth collection opens with the first of ten full-colour illustrations in which we find the devil "guiding (the poet's) hand, trickling words in her ear." These collages possess the same "scratchy folk-art feel" as handmade puppets in the Museum of Witchcraft. In concert with the thistly tones of the poems they interlace, the artworks offer a different texture to the sophisticated, bomb-proof forms in which Ivory gives voice to a chorus of history's weirdest wayward women, as in 'The Waking':

> – why must we be occult? I hold
> up those rekindled women and we reel, we howl, and we
> shoot our filthy mouths off

No word is wasted here as Ivory persuasively assembles the subversive history of the woman-as-witch. From supernatural rites to abortion rights, these poems are alive to failed "due process in court(s) of law" ('Prick') that have demonised the women who labour, care or survive. A shocking 2% of medical research funding is globally spent on pregnancy, childbirth, and reproductive health each year (*New Scientist*, 2024). '34 Symptoms of the Menopause' tackles this statistic head-on, as "At 3am, a woman Googles burning tongue" whilst another's body "feels like a bee box too small for the bees".

This impressive collection tackles the fear and denigration of ageing women whilst advocating for a womanhood that is as "mutable as the day is long" ('More thoughts about the body'). Ivory skilfully balances upon the knife's edge between disentangling the patriarchal weaponisation of the occult and honouring the saving graces of a feminist coven, as the new lyric testimony given to Pendle's Margaret Johnson epitomises:

> Yet history casts me out as *not a witch* –
> if I was *not* a witch,
> how did I meet the night's wings? how did I fly?

JO CLEMENT

HELEN IVORY

I started out on this path two Bloodaxe books ago. The autobiographical *Waiting for Bluebeard* (2013) centres on domestic abuse and *The Anatomical Venus* (2019) emerged from conversations I had with women about their own "Bluebeards". We were gaslit and convinced there was something wrong with us. We were made to feel "other" and controlled. Related to this is the treatment of women in society down through history and I saw how my own story became part of a wider picture. The archetype of a woman gone wrong is the witch, so the witch became my lens.

Constructing a Witch begins with an extract from Scold's Bridle (*The Anatomical Venus*). Both an object of torture and a metaphor – a way to rupture the tongue of a troublesome woman. There is one in the Museum of Witchcraft in Boscastle. I decided I wanted to explore what led to the smithery of this object and then to try to understand why and how women have been silenced, monstered and othered. I wanted to explore female power and disempowerment. My investigations spanned from *The Malleus Maleficarum* to *The Wizard of Oz* and importantly took me to the places where those accused of witchcraft were murdered.

This is a research-based book as well as a deeply personal one. The witch is a symbol of ageing femininity, which I have been researching in the field of late. She enabled me to think about the politics of the female body including the menopause. With the collage/poems – this way of working always feels alchemic to me; the magical process of transformation and creation. When making collage from pre-existing materials, each thing that you use is already charged with its own power. Words also carry things over from all their past lives – a kind of magical process or quantum entanglement, if you will.

HELEN RECOMMENDS

Moniza Alvi, *Bye Bye Blackbird* (Bloodaxe Books); Eds. Cassandra Atherton and Oz Hardwick, *Dancing about Architecture and Other Ekphrastic Maneuvers* (MadHat); Jean Atkin, *High Nowhere* (Indigo Dreams); Rachel Curzon, *Faber New Poets 16* (Faber); Martin Figura, *The Remaining Men* (Cinnamon); Matt Howard, *Broadlands* (Bloodaxe); Camille Ralphs, *Malkin* (Emma Press); Elisabeth Sennitt Clough, *my name is abilene* (Salt); Clare Shaw, *Towards a General Theory of Love* (Bloodaxe); Charles Simic, *Dimestore Alchemy* (New York Review Books); Toon Tellegen, *Raptors,* trans. Judith Wilkinson (Carcanet); Julia Webb, *Threat* (Nine Arches Press).

By the slant of her tone,

you will see the narrator

cuts desire lines with a scalpel.

Turn back now if you fear the devil

is at play on the cutting mat –

guiding her hand, trickling words in her ear.

For, oh she is the weaker vessel;

the devil's gateway to your thirsty hothouse.

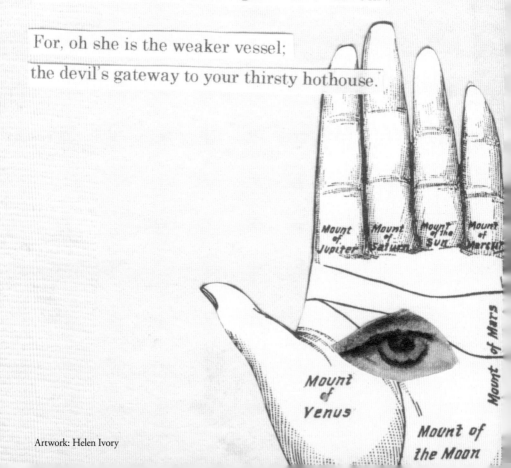

Mount
of
Jupiter

Mount
of
Saturn

Mount
of the
Sun

Mount
of
Mercury

Mount of Mars

Mount
of
Venus

Mount of
the Moon

Artwork: Helen Ivory

WOULDST THOU LIKE TO LIVE DELICIOUSLY?

BLACK PHILLIP: The VVitch, 2015

I have marked you
at the gateway to the forest
inhaling the wildwood like medicine.

And I have sent the most velvet of hares
as a gift of my heart
to usher you from the burdensome world.

You have been the pious daughter –
washed your father's rags in the brook.
Have you not earnt enough of god's grace?

Your parents bade you pray for light
while heaping shadows round your character.
Harken as they brand you *witch*, without a lick of proof.

Come follow, I have such bounty for you.
There is always a little bloodshed
when a woman is born.

RUTH PADEL

Ruth Padel has won the National Poetry Competition and published twelve acclaimed poetry collections, including *We Are All from Somewhere Else,* on animal and human migration, and popular books on reading poetry. Her recent novel *Daughters of the Labyrinth*, shortlisted for the Anglo-Hellenic and Runciman Prizes, turned on the Holocaust in Crete, where she used to live. She has also published much-praised non-fiction on Greek tragedy, the influence of Greek myth on rock music, and wild tiger conservation. She is currently writing a book on elephants and is a Fellow of the Zoological Society of London and the Royal Society of Literature.

SPECIAL COMMENDATION

GIRL

CHATTO & WINDUS | £12.99 | PBS PRICE £9.72

"One is not born, but rather becomes, woman," writes Simone de Beauvoir in *The Second Sex*. In these intimate portrayals of goddesses and girlhood, Ruth Padel's blazing new collection *Girl* examines the "state of inferiority" imposed by a ranked gender binary. 'When the Angel Comes for You' recasts the immaculate conception as rape, in which a red-eyed dove preys upon and abandons Mary, "plugged with gold / vibrating to bells". In Padel's modern-day nativity, Mary holds her newborn fearfully, as moonlight scatters through a bubbling water cooler, casting "pearls on the floor" ('Barn'). Christ's passion soon becomes his mother's, as a litany of punishing injuries imposed by flick knives and falls converge with snapshots from the poet's own life. Written after Czesław Miłosz, 'The Crowd Around your Child' extends these tortures to ongoing injustices in "Syria / Ukraine / Gaza":

> We think we can keep ourselves apart from the flames
> but they're everywhere
> every hour inside us again and then again

The sequence 'Lady of the Labyrinth' examines how Sir Arthur Evans distorted knowledge of Minoan goddesses. Wearing a funereal black brocade, one such goddess responds to both the liberties Evans took in restoring archaeological statues and the question, "Why do men want / to see naked girls fooling with snakes?":

> Having died she tells me,
> all the way back to the root, I grow again.
> The serpent of the unconscious

An outstanding triptych with adventurous forms and striking sounds, *Girl* swings from prehistory to the present day. Unafraid to "square up to the Minotaur / in his white colonial pith helmet"('Until I Thought of Myself as Ariadne') and the ruinous "images men have made", Padel is a sensitive poet eager to toast peace, pleasure and equality. I am with her every step of the way.

> Ariadne I don't want
> a sword. Just your thread
> and the dancing will do.

SELECTOR'S COMMENT

JO CLEMENT

PHOTOS FROM UNDER THE BED

I pull them out of a suitcase
spit-curls of myself

cloudy
proof of girls
I have been

maybe still am
and think of a dipterocarp
seed on the rainforest floor

a wee scrotum self
how it unfurls

how it steps forward
choosing to risk
lose   explore.

Little soul
you have wandered a long time
and now see a door

standing open.
At night

the bloop of a text
lights up the cell-phone
rousting me from sleep

asking me to click
these ruby slippers
that have somehow blossomed on my feet.

yes now I look back
it was all explore.

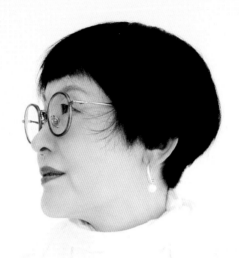
Image: Jung Melmel

Image: Song Got

KIM HYESOON

DON MEE CHOI

Kim Hyesoon, born in 1955, is one of the most prominent and influential contemporary poets of South Korea. She was the first woman poet to receive the prestigious Kim Su-yong and Midang awards. Kim recently received the 2019 International Griffin Poetry Prize for *Autobiography of Death* and the Samsung Ho-Am Prize in 2022. Her poetry has been translated into Chinese, French, German, Japanese, Spanish, Danish, and Swedish.

Born in Seoul, South Korea, Don Mee Choi is the author of the National Book Award winning collection *DMZ Colony* (Wave Books, 2020), *Hardly War* (Wave Books, 2016), *The Morning News Is Exciting* (Action Books, 2010), pamphlets and essays. She has received a Guggenheim Fellowship, MacArthur Fellowship, Whiting Award, Lannan Literary Fellowship, Lucien Stryk Translation Prize, and DAAD Artists-in-Berlin Fellowship. She has translated several collections of Kim Hyesoon's poetry.

PHANTOM PAIN WINGS
KIM HYESOON, TRANS. DON MEE CHOI
AND OTHER STORIES | £14.99 | PBS PRICE £11.24

Phantom
Pain
Wings

Kim Hyesoon

¶ This book is not really a book ¶
It's an I-do-bird sequence ¶ a record
of the sequence ¶¶ When I take off
my shoes. stand on the railing ¶ and
spread my arms with eyes closed ¶
feathers poke out of my sleeves ¶ Bird-
cries-out-from-me-day record ¶ I-do-
bird-day record¶ as I caress bird's
cheeks…*Translated by Don Mee Choi*

When is a writer a woman, and when is she a bird? In Kim Hyesoon's *Phantom Pain Wings*, translated from the Korean by Don Mee Choi, the answer is both, at all times. The answer, too, is behind you, wearing a bloody smile, dwelling in the ephemeral and the scatological, soaring between planes of the absurd and the utterly gut-wrenching. If this is your first encounter with Hyesoon, expect to be riven by sensation – expect what floods into your apertures to resound with grief, to pulse with all its ungovernable anatomies.

Across four poem sections and an essay, in itself starkly poetic, the speakers are pursued by birds, and enact upon themselves all stations and carnalities of birdhood. This living with, and living through, the bird as companion and consummate beloved, transcends what we normatively call a "relationship": the birds and human animals in these poems do more than abide with each other. They subsume. They replicate patterns, spiralling and defecating. They devour. In the book's first poem, 'Bird's Poetry Book', the speaker cradles and transmits a failing language between themselves and the vessel, which is bird:

> Bird has shrunken enough to be cupped in my hands
> Bird mumbles something incomprehensible even when my lips touch its
> beak

Cyclically, the poet's mischievous, shell-shocked and transgressive speakers return to the impossibility of language to capture all this: the mania of bereavement; the spectacle of mourning; the inscrutability of the heart's most chthonic desires. Don Mee Choi, who has been translating Hyesoon for over a decade, occupies a role in the text that feels like far more than linguistic intermediary. Her "Translator's Diary", appearing at the end of the book, allows us into the perforations and silences housed in the language itself, murmuring between Korean and English.

Cravers of an unutterable intimacy will find it in *Phantom Pain Wings* – here, all the knives are feathered, and flying with contrails of blood.

SHIVANEE RAMLOCHAN

GOING GOING GONE

Bird cuts me out
like the way sunlight cuts out shadows

Hole enters
the spot where I was cut out
I exit

Bird cuts me out
like the way time cuts me

Gaping mouth enters
the cutout

I exit through the open mouth
then return as a deformed child

I exit again

I take a step toward where I don't exist

I take a step toward where I don't exist

Bird doesn't cut me out
Behind the wall I'm on standby forever

MORAG SMITH

Morag Smith was born in Cornwall on the 24th March 1969. She grew up in Essex and on the Isle of Lewis. She had six children and nine grandchildren. She lived for a number of years as a New Age Traveller with her then young family. She returned to Cornwall and graduated from the University of Falmouth in 2019 with a First Class Degree in Creative Writing. She was a member of the Falmouth Poetry Group, and engaged widely with the poetry community in Cornwall. Morag was also an artist, a Zen Buddhist, and an activist, working notably with the Clean Ocean Trust. She died on the 26th July 2023, having received a terminal cancer diagnosis in March of that year.

NATIONAL SONG

BROKEN SLEEP BOOKS | £9.99 |

National Song by Morag Smith is a collection that immediately draws in its reader. Fearless and poignant, these poems click into place with enviable ease. That place, for me, is located in the heart; I feel the pleasure of reading these poems in bodily pangs and twinges. I take in a sharp breath at lines that unpredictably, sombrely, and yet exquisitely, liken a formation of birds to the military; my body clenches when Smith searches for an irretrievable sense of self among the fragments of nations marked by colonialism; I feel myself relax when the poem at last articulates its difficulty, voicing with remarkable lyricism what might be an unease with borders, an overall perplexity with the concept of a national song at all.

> if I belong anywhere it's in the lee of a mountain I've never seen

In a sense, these poems stir our imaginations with exact and striking images of the land. Smith casts her lens on flora and fauna of the natural world, treading a history of occupation and a spectrum of violence across time and space. She makes one particular story of intergenerational trauma legible by tracing the ecological, and so, anemone, geese, thistle, heather, and a "stream of dark birds" become symbolic of an experience of place, of womanhood, of language.

> on the sands of Ictis
> a figure stands silhouetted by sunrise
> one moment an empty horizon
> the next there were boats
> a thousand years ago you came
> back then I was warrior   woman
> you cut the earth   saw my blood flow
> to the narrow beach   onto the stones
> clots of my life shiny as anemones

The thrill – the surprise and skill of these poems – lies in how they turn. In the possibility that opens when an image transforms, when its own borders become porous, allowing narratives to co-mingle, to reach far and wide and land in spaces of new and unexpected understandings.

SELECTOR'S COMMENT

46   YOUSIF M. QASMIYEH & ALYCIA PIRMOHAMED

ANXIOUS

Caught in the bone cage
startled birds
beat fast wings
against my fragile lungs
breathing is strange
air is hard to take
it hums

the tongue
pushes against a fish-bone pallet
the face hums
the body becomes transparent
impossible to hide inside
the rib rack holds too many birds
crushing them slowly to stillness
wings lock into each other
beady eyes strain sideways
unable to focus
feathered frames hold hearts
that echo through their hollow bones
my chest conceals them
and their panic grows
can't sing
can't fly
eyes pressed into each other's eyes

I open my mouth
releasing a stream

of dark birds
into the light

WINTER BOOK REVIEWS

JUANA ADCOCK: I SUGAR THE BONES
REVIEWED BY DAVE COATES

The Mexican-born, Glasgow-based poet's second English collection is jaw-droppingly deft, switching seamlessly between artful tableaux, wry monologues and lyric essays. These poems are journeys of a sensitive, insightful and witty mind at work, whether negotiating colonialism and labour rights via the Spanish-language actors of The Simpsons and Sailor Moon, or offering a heartfelt, surrealist ode to the River Clyde. Few books balance such omnivorous curiosity with such a consistency of focus and aesthetic quality.

OUTSPOKEN PRESS | £11.99 | PBS PRICE £9.00

DZIFA BENSON: MONSTER
REVIEWED BY SHALINI SENGUPTA

This devastatingly strong, tender and complex debut features an unflinching study of Sarah Baartman – a South African Khoikhoi woman displayed in "freak" shows in 19th century Europe. Benson refracts "monstrosity" into something beyond words: something that scrapes, interrogates, and humbles. With moving emotional heft and stark storytelling, Benson explores Black female subjectivity and the tension between the brutal and poignant. This is a hypnotic book which makes you feel uncomfortable, the way all good poetry should.

BLOODAXE BOOKS | £12.99 | PBS PRICE £9.72

JAMES BYRNE: THE OVERMIND
REVIEWED BY SHASH TREVETT

The seventh collection from this acclaimed poet is "fractalised" with poems, like puzzle pieces, which join together to make a whole. Ranging from tender poems about his daughter and father, to poems which dismantle power (the monarchy, colonialism, the Tory government during the pandemic), and others in celebration of those who have inspired him, this is a book which makes the reader think. An exquisite collection excavating time and memory in poems hung "from a hole on the wind's back" as an offering to the reader.

BROKEN SLEEP BOOKS | £12.99 | PBS PRICE £9.72

LEDBURY CRITICS

ED. JO CLEMENT: THRESHOLDS
REVIEWED BY SHASH TREVETT

Emerging from the Brown Girls Write programme set up by Sharmin Islam at New Writing North, this anthology of eleven exciting new South Asian voices crosses thresholds, unapologetically, to occupy a space of its own. Examining family life, religion, love, visibility and the female body, these are sophisticated poems playing with rhyme, form, history and geography with a musicality which flows off the page. A new generation speaks, reclaiming not just the brown of their bodies, but digging deeper to expose threads of gold.

BUTCHER'S DOG | £10.99 | PBS PRICE £8.25

WILL EAVES: INVASION OF THE POLYHEDRONS
REVIEWED BY SHASH TREVETT

A collection which feels like a gathering together from a long and rich career. Eaves excavates the living landscape in poems which keep "the menace of a grey mid-morning" at bay. These are deeply satisfying to read, revealing quiet and solitary truths without fanfare. The collection also contains prose work by Eaves: an essay on Auden, a couple of reviews and a poignant letter of farewell to an old friend, which opens a window into the soul of this acclaimed writer.

CB EDITIONS | £10.99 | PBS PRICE £8.25

SAMATAR ELMI: THE EPIC OF CADER IDRIS
REVIEWED BY SHALINI SENGUPTA

This collection is such a powerhouse. Elmi's work is as surreal as it is sinister, and these poems read like tender but knowing observations of a world in constant flux. There is so much luscious, expansive imagery in this collection. I'm floored by the description of diaspora as a "gift and a curse" and the interrogation of home, birthplace, and belonging, as torturous, violent, and melancholic. The lines, "it is we who are the instruments strummed by our losses that wait by the window" brings a lump to my throat every time.

FLIPPED EYE | £18.95 | PBS PRICE £14.22 (HARDBACK)

BOOK REVIEWS

ADALBER SALAS HERNÁNDEZ: ISOLARIO/ISLARIUM
REVIEWED BY DAVE COATES

Translated by Robin Myers, *Isolario/Islarium* skilfully fits content to form: each prose poem is a self-contained stopping point. From ancient China to the poet's native Venezuela, Salas Hernández applies a surreal and soulful imagination to the stories that islands have inspired: places of infinite possibility subject to the imperial impulse to possess the unknowable. Though the book occasionally loses its bearings in odd voyages, the poet's curiosity and energy are infectious, and connections drawn between childhood memory and adult inquiry are powerfully rendered.

PEEPAL TREE PRESS | £10.99 | PBS PRICE £8.25

AMAAN HYDER: SELF PORTRAIT WITH FAMILY
REVIEWED BY SHALINI SENGUPTA

Hyder opens with a sense of free-fall juxtaposed against a series of public and private stops – the obstruction of desire, language, and identity during "stop-start days" in London. Each poem offers a glimpse into family, diaspora, queerness and orbits despair, isolation, connection and rebellion. I love the anticipatory temporality in this work: the periodic cruising towards a dream future. This book is one I will return to when I am finding it hard to allow myself to accept a difficult feeling. This collection is a permission.

NINE ARCHES PRESS | £11.99 | PBS PRICE £9.00

MIMI KHALVATI: COLLECTED POEMS
REVIEWED BY DAVE COATES

Since her 1990 debut, Khalvati has unassumingly transformed British poetry, as a masterful lyricist and founder of the Poetry School. Her work is faithful to its odd instincts and passions, a skilful painter of the idiosyncratic, resonant image. Her moving elegy for Michael Donaghy references Lorca's theory of the duende, art's capacity to draw strength from the jaws of death. Khalvati's duende is quiet, precise, humane, unshakeable, and observing her career as it evolves in this volume is a privilege.

CARCANET PRESS | £30.00 | PBS PRICE £25.00

McAuliffe's sixth collection is a miscellany, a meandering and often amusing tour through the poet's day-to-day, with a jaundiced eye toward contemporary politics that informs the best poem in the book 'The Border Shuts' a wry curse of Brexit and the DUP. Too many poems, however, feel unfocused, or incomplete, or spend too much energy nodding towards other writers and artists to explore their own imaginative or philosophical horizons. Still, *National Theatre* is a solid, thoughtful diary from a seasoned veteran.

GALLERY PRESS | £9.97 | PSB PRICE £7.32

Mingle offers an insight into what poetry can achieve when the mind is completely unharnessed. Drawing epigraphs from Frank O'Hara to Britney Spears: this surprising co-mingling of voices makes for a perfect union. Written with O'Hara's knack for evoking people, places, and objects: these poems are urbane and rooted in the everyday. Parkin's mischievous humour and lush, environmentally conscious imagery are bestowed with a hint of otherworldliness. A healthy snack to immortalise your soul.

NINE ARCHES PRESS | £11.99 | PBS PRICE £9.00

ERICA GILLINGHAM

JEM HENDERSON

JP SEABRIGHT

Intellectually luminous and deeply affecting, *Motherflux* makes a case for radical, liberated, and collective care. The figure of the "mother" fades in and out, is dismantled and turned on its head. This is a triumphant portrait of queer parenthood: of being a "girlboy mumdad" and the "other mother / the unnatural one". The writers light up entire worlds in brief sequences: their linguistic dance stems from astute observations and shatters your heart very, very softly. I hope everyone reads this collection.

NINE PENS PRESS | £7.50 | PBS PRICE £5.25

BOOK REVIEWS

NIA BROOMHALL: BACKALONG
REVIEWED BY MEGAN ROBSON

This achingly beautiful pamphlet, winner of the 2023 Mslexia Women's Pamphlet Competition, introduces Nia Broomhall as a talent to watch. Her poetry thrills with rich sound and colour-scapes, paying tribute to Broomhall's native Somerset, to family, and to absent friends; most notably Nina, to whom the pamphlet is dedicated. Grief is keenly present here, but so is the determination to hold on to the future, painful though it may be: "I will plant them / anyway. She will still be / gone."

BLOODAXE BOOKS   £7.50

FRED D'AGUIAR: GHOST PARTICLES

Written with deep admiration and affection for his childhood English teacher at Charlton Boys Secondary School, Fred D'Aguiar's *Ghost Particles* is a memorial for Geoff Hardy, a great supporter of the arts and the LGBT community: "I think how you figure / in my life in myriad ways". These poems centre around that deeply relatable pain of losing someone formative in your life and trying to word them back into being, "wide-spread arms / embrace you."

FAIR ACRE PRESS   £7.50

ANETA KAMIŃSKA: CZERNOVITZ-CHARMOVITZ
REVIEWED BY MEGAN ROBSON

This powerful selection of work traces the career of Aneta Kamińska through her writing on femininity and sexuality, on urban living and the Covid-19 pandemic, and the war in Ukraine. The introduction from translators Anna Blasiak and Bohdan Piasecki highlights the difficulties and joys of translating a poet whose main tools include wordplay and neologisms. *Czernovitz-Charmovitz* recognises a unique poet, and allows the reader a glimpse into the process of translating poetry which engages with linguistic innovation.

ARC PUBLICATIONS   £8.00